CW00739088

there's no such thing

lily blacksell

ignitionpress

For my family

First published in 2018
by **ignition**press
Oxford Brookes Poetry Centre
Oxford Brookes University
OX3 0BP

Cover design: Flora Hands, Carline Creative
Page design: Thomas Nicolaou

A CIP record for this book is available from the British Library

ISBN 978-9997412-3-5

Contents

*footsteps whose sound
is my heart souped up*

Thylias Moss

Girl Reaction

Thinking about it makes me mad and I mean it
in both senses of the word, not because I was
fourteen years old and just about out of my mind
with esteem, or because the burger-van man
said he didn't like my sunglasses, or because
someone behind me in the crowd threw a cup
of his piss at my head, shouting out I was too tall.
I loved those glasses and there's no such thing.
I hardly noticed because on stage there was
so clearly something wrong and it's maddening,
exactly how literal is the inferno inferred by
hell of a show? How much did it all take out of her,
and how much did we give back? When she returned
in the Stones' set to sing Ain't Too Proud to Beg
with Mick, she must have known hundreds of thousands
could hear her, in tune, in time, in need, in jeans
and a t-shirt and beehive and it's mad and I mean it
that he once declared he'd rather be dead
than singing Satisfaction at forty. At seventy-four
he still won't shut up. She was only asking us to leave
her alone, singing to and by herself, but we never did,
she never was, she never got no

The Ballad of Standing a Chance

I went to the party in a backless top I mean
it kind of had no spine and it looked good with jeans
and the lipstick I put on was new in a colour
called Modesty which actually suited me well

and it turned out the venue was a film-set that looked like
a street on which all of the buildings were derelict
and when everyone's dying it's de rigueur to be late
so in that sense I made quite an entrance at which point

Fru-Fru explained it wasn't just her birthday
she was leaving for good as soon as she could
and that's why the banner said So Long! Farewell!
doubling up as a von Trapp/Anschluss reference

she had asked the baker to come with a cake
but he told her that he couldn't make it
and somebody had texted both their dealers that day
but they said they just couldn't take it

so she'd been stuffing pills into fortune cookies
which you could get at the fake Chinese restaurant
and the salt in the chip shop was actually cocaine
and people were willingly drinking the vinegar

which meant more room at the bar for me and my one friend
the epileptic orphan Sixpenny Crick with a fez on his head
and a Freud finger puppet and a long list of ailments topped
with Type1 diabetes and carrying on from there

(he passed away not long after the party and left my family
a case of his wine so he must have known we would still
be on our feet we would still be on our feet with our shoes
worn through and no good to us) eventually I got too cold

at the party what with the wind dancing round my bare kidneys
and all of the alcohol gone and the fake off-licence imagine
a fuck off licence imagine if we all had one of those now
and I took myself home on the assumption I still had one

and I discovered my housemate laid flat on the floor
he tapped out his heartbeat on my left leg for me
a sign of affection I have no doubt but I couldn't help
noticing how erratic it was and all in a figure of eight no kidding

I went outside to flag down a helicopter only to see
every rope ladder had been cut and suddenly I felt
not very fantastic so switched on our music and disco ball
to drown out the sirens to refract the searchlights

and I joined him on the carpet and we made it through the night
(I gave that away already with the talk of our feet of our feet) except
at dawn I found my heart had gone and broken leaving the gate open
which is why my pulse was slamming which is why it would not shut

We are to blame for the decline
of giraffes and only we can save them

Read the headlines aloud to your partner in
bed when your love life is losing momentum.

Tear the phone from his hands, the wool from his eyes
shake his shoulders, repeat 'don't you see?'

Get ready to go and decide on the spot
if, realistically, you'll have time

for breakfast. Nothing has ever mattered
more than this. Perhaps you'll pick something up

on the way. Don't be surprised if and when he says
'Wait, will you? Wait. I don't think I'm coming.'

It'll hit with the precision of a kick
in the teeth, if a round-toed boot

was the kicker. Sad, really, when that's just the sort
of shoe you would want to help a giraffe in.

Put down your backpack, then think better of it
and pick up your backpack again.

Say nothing, because what could come out of the blue
of your swollen mouth, empty stomach

and dumbness? Rip a wafer thin extract
of yourself and swallow. Remember to pack

lip balm, sun-cream, two apples and a plum.
Breathe if possible and learn your ceiling:

lightbulb, damp patch, crack. Absolutely, yes,
I bet he'll say 'look at me', but you mustn't,

do you hear? This is worse than him ogling
his ex's stupid beautiful photos,

this is worse than breaking your noble heart.
This time, it's global, you told him, it's urgent,

there are nine islands of giraffes left in the wild.
But he'd be aware if he'd been listening.

Say nothing, because all you know now
for certain is lightbulb, damp patch, crack,

and he won't understand. You should turn on your heel
and go to your brother's. You've missed your brother so much.

If he asks any questions, tell him you wanted
different things (you can say that again)

with regard to the giraffes and without,
but he won't ask any questions, you know.

Ain't Nothing Like the Real Thing

I like being told what time it is
always thinking to myself
no it isn't and I like being told
what the weather will do knowing
very well that it won't. It does wonders
for one's acceptance and once I was put
at the same desk as an old flame at work
and the silence was really something
and he asked if he could play some music
and in the end I beat him to it because
I can type at great speed if needs be.
Oh Aretha Franklin! I said by mistake
when it loaded when it was really
The Staple Singers and I felt foolish
but he didn't seem to notice or care
which should tell you all you need to know.
This was probably one of the good songs
and the stoic in me suffers the bad
songs in return and the magpie steals
the phrasing of the DJs and all
their celebrity guests and if my language
is a linden or lime tree then this
must be the sap and the leaves
and I can't do it on my own and I don't
have to. I'd just like to say that that
aforementioned flame was so old
not even a spoon could have stirred it
nor could a litre of petrol
so don't get distracted. We mustn't
forget Freddie Mercury used to sing
Radio someone still loves you meaning
himself but Fred is dead and the biopic
is not looking hopeful but Radio it'll be ok

someone else still loves you
and I know all the words and the tune.
A friend from home who works in radio
told me the best way to get your song
played on the radio is to write a song
about the radio. Keep your fingers crossed
for me because this is the best I've got.
Then I suppose there are all the times
I've been declared a good listener.
To be perfectly honest it's true.

Meanwhile back at the ranch

I insisted on taking down the coat hangers
dangling empty by the end of the day because they made me think
of gin in a bathtub which is not the way to drink it. This just hours
after I'd done a test quietly in the Ladies on the ferry. I knew
I'd cry on that crossing so it was only one more or less reason to.

I don't think other people have done that before because
it wasn't the time or the place but they say don't they
that you should keep your eyes on the horizon
something about the steady line that you look for
after a minute has come and gone (like a man! maybe!) so if
it wasn't the time it was the time eventually and if
it wasn't the place either I was on my way elsewhere.

I do hope the chemist's ok because he looked quite upset.
I don't think he sells very many. I'm proud of myself
for not buying a flannel and trying to cover it up
or beating around the bush (excuse me).

I was there for a reason one reason alone. I'd knocked out
a wing mirror earlier and couldn't have looked back if I'd wanted to.
I only dared change lanes to the right. There's been a lot of that
happening recently I think. I come from a long line of car crashes
owing to rare-breed cows and Harvey Nick's Christmas window displays.

We will always turn to better see Belted Galloways grazing.
They look like panda bears. They charge to protect their young.
Meanwhile back at the café by which I mean Irving Farm a man
is reading aloud from Beloved and a woman is reading
(in her head) Raising Competent Children. You couldn't
make it up as they say don't they.

Sparrow's Kneecaps

Please believe me in full when
I say it was only after
we'd tried everything else
(I've tried everything!
I've tried everything!
as Annie Lennox once, twice,
more than that, told us) we drilled
a hole into my mother's head.

The faraway look   arrived
in her eyes, set them somewhat
swimming, but out of their depth
so we hurried her upstairs
(I took wrists, George took ankles)
and into dad's pyjamas before
the worst of the terrible
weather began   coming in.

To our surprise, the fontanelle
was not hard to find, not
hard at all, but re-softened
and scary   as though the role
reversal   had taken its toll
already.   Something to do
with the German for dream
and not enough hours in a week

day baby baby baby
My Babies Just Care for Me
for her own good, which lost all
meaning twenty-eight or so
years ago when her goods became
our goods too and twice over
they cut her body in two
and this the thanks she gets.

All women are berated
equal   in a variety
of different ways but bear
in mind the first rule of Plight Club:
bad workwomen blame their tools.
Her mother kept mum during
the electric shock treatment
to stun her (already stunning)

into parenthood once and
for all and again.   By the end
her hair stood up like barley
and she gave all her Elnett
away. She was still smoking
in those days and as she rose
from the table/bed she was
faintly smoking too I suppose

and as the family saying goes:
'I smell burning! I smell burning!'
when a mother starts to martyr
herself by giving us extra pudding
or something   or offering
to do the food shop or homework
tying herself to the stake
with one hand, lighting the match

with the other, all the while
patting our heads with her feet
and trying her best to make
enough phone calls and doing
her darnedest with a profound
deep distrust   for the body
she must do to as she would be
done by.   The Victorians

swore by it, just like heaven,
but still it seemed excessive
to drill, to risk a mistake
when we had no real trepan,
when there was no bone to break.
George fetched the Bosch, meanwhile
I drew the curtains and held
her hand, said oh don't be daft

we'll buy you more hats, you will
quite like the draught, we won't let
the rain get in there, just fresh air
your poor head won't hurt any more.
There now, there now, there now, there
count backwards with me from tender, tender, tenderer
I can't begin to tell you

Who cares for the feeling of feeling alone

Thursday's child is a first class pipsqueak with an Elmo book called
I Love You This Much which is a lot more forthcoming than the book
I grew up with called Guess How Much I Love You. When I read
her I Love You This Much I wind up telling her I love you in twenty
different ways three times in a row and listen, she's a great little kid,
musical, calm and charming, but I've only known her a month or so
and I'm coming over all Barrett Browning. My boyfriend had no such
luck. He was one of those kept guessing.

                                       Boney Maloney,
if you're reading this, sometimes your hip against my inner thigh
hurt, but it was no one's fault. I can do naked, do incessant affection,
do sensitivity, excitability mounting but your talk of the future made
my heart sink not sing. I borrowed the book and said it over coffee
I love you in twenty different ways three times in a row and listen
it's not like me, this seriousness. It's a sign of the times, now we panic
in a worldly way and our anxiety, in its enormity, is continental and
besides that nickname is bad. I only just thought of it now.

                                   My yoga teacher told me to relax
my jaw and all of a sudden I was in Anomalisa. How about that,
Charlie Kaufman, my mouth is nothing but a mechanism
and I sincerely think it might fall apart any day now. Both my rickety
puppetry knees will buckle and then the motion will stop. She says
shake your head yes and no very good we'll meet again in downward
facing dog and it is very good I agree it's effective but she's telling us
what to think and that puts me in mind of when

                              I was in Southampton last year, waiting for the ferry,
I'M IN sticker on my jacket. A fisherman saw it and spat at me, asking
if I was in the Illuminati, if I was happy. I don't know what Illuminati is,
I've always assumed it's to do with Beyoncé. My toddler friend
has an Elmo toy and a Cookie Monster toy known as Blue Elmo.
That's beautiful. That's all we are when it comes down to it, not so

different. As I patted my sticker and dabbed at the mucus sliding down my chest with my sleeve I was Blue Elmo in spirit but blushing like mad singing Dobie Gray in a whisper, I'm in with the in crowd do do do do.

When you're in with the in crowd, it's so easy to find romance. A pheasant lived in our garden for so long we called him Geoffrey. This was before I'd even heard of Christopher Smart and considering how many months Geoffrey spent strutting around the stargazer, he must have missed multiple mating seasons, not to mention men with guns. Wherever he went in the end, I hope it was of natural causes. I hope he knew he was leaving for the first and only time. A lot of the birdwatchers in the village keep a rifle alongside their binoculars. It's not that they're short-sighted, hypocritical and risky or maybe that's exactly it. I'll have to ask my yoga teacher for an efficacious way to tell them

because I've realised I am too polite to say almost anything. Saving up for a Tammy t-shirt that said What Attitude Problem? does not mean I ever had an attitude problem. To this day, I sign my emails thank you, hold the door to let the cold in and only speak ill of the dead when spoken to. This week, my aunt let us know she is dying in an email entitled Death. She's beaten cancer twice before so it's hardly her first rodeo but the doctors and body of the email seem to think it'll be her last. I'm sending her a card addressed c/o The Pickled Parrot because she lives there. This isn't a Monty Python thing. If you aren't laughing yet it's quite likely you never will. I am hoping not to cry next weekend, so that's something to look forward to. I'll be feasting on Gordon's gin and fish-sticks and when all the tulips collapse the moment I put them in water I'm not going to take it personally. I'm not going to let it get to me. The last thing I'm going to do is stop buying myself flowers.

The Stirrups

for Madeline DeFrees

The confusion started years ago
with her mother's use of the same
gentle metaphor to describe
breakups and falls from horses.
Both were cases of 'coming adrift'.

Furthermore, her mother taught her
how to ride and not to reach her hand out
if she fell. It would break her wrist
for certain. 'Try to wrap your arms
around yourself, darling, relax!'

Years later, on getting pregnant
she had tried to do just that.
'Lie down,' they said, 'and we'll treat you.'
Her then-boyfriend got hotdogs (comfort food)
for the long drive home from the clinic.

She didn't want them and choice was
her prerogative. He asked how she felt,
she said stirred and sore, nothing more,
to cheer her up he played 'Stir It Up'
she got the joke and took it lying down.

Years before, she and her horse came adrift
when he shied and bolted (what to expect
when you're not) and she broke her collarbone
when she fell (correctly), strait-jacketed
in her own embrace, dragged along because

her foot was caught in the iron,
spitting blood and dirt and half a tooth,
crying out the horse's human name,
saying woah saying steady saying stop.
Her foot came loose and she lay still.

The night rode out to meet her. The horse
galloped all the way home, alone,
snorting, sweating, bewildering.
Her mother grabbed his reins, tugged his mane,
cried 'where is she, darling, what happened?'

These days, her dear mother long gone,
she thinks about the ghost of something
that mattered, and whether or not it did.
She reads about Republicans
who want to ban abortions.

She reads about Democrats
who want to ban the carriages
in Central Park: it's apparently
a question of quality of life.
There's an old grey mare on Broadway,

the first horse she has seen in so long.
David Foster Wallace says their heads
are shaped like coffins, somehow.
She has a look, he has a point, but no
one, nobody, could need a coffin that small.

Rocinante is no name for a skateboard

I know that chivalry is still alive
because men are falling at my feet.
The thud of one comes up through my heels
when I think of him hitting the floor:
a skid that became a wince-hiss of pain.
I blushed for him and again for the blindness
of strangers, hoped he'd stand up and dust it off,
not say I'm ok, as though I'd asked.
That morning I bet he'd reached for his knee pads,
then thought not today, I've improved,
and lowered slowly into his bath that night,
flinching at the sting, or the prospect of it.
The sound of his backside against his tub
slides slowly down the side of my head.

Loose Lips

A cormorant diving nearby at the time couldn't help
couldn't help but notice all the sea's salt and all the cold water

cold water did not remove the rust-red stains from her skirts
her skirts whirled like turmoil around her neck and head her knickers

first bloomed then flattened and stayed where they were
with arms outstretched as if to keep her balance she looked

she looked almost ready for anything and her mouth wide open
wide open and covered over with petticoat was only agape

for her sigh of relief and the bird had never seen bubbles so
so so elegant before and he had never seen such dry blood

You can't just do that

If there's enough blue in the sky to make a sailor's pair
of trousers, it isn't going to rain again today.
Is that the sort of promise that got you into this mess, deario?
In the first place, with your easel, with your tent without its poles.

Blue is the colour of the denim on the shoulder that I drooled on
when I found you on the kindly night bus home.
You made a radio show for it all, I texted in every week–
did you see my messages, get my jokes, think highly of my requests

as you thought highly during your time on the road and sent me
texts that made no sense and made me worry/wonder
if it's that sort of habit that got you into this mess, old sport.
With friends like you, who needs lurking maternity. My soft spot

for drummers started with you, throwing stones through
big old car windows. 'You look like her,' you said, finger on a picture
of Emma Watson, and I thought you might be more than colour-blind.
Forget about he for she for now, chum. Get well, get home

soon. Just like we managed, even without foglights, after the blind
mole's ball. I didn't know how to use them and you were in charge
of the music. Whenever I see dead leaves on the dirty ground
it makes me think of you, because Dead Leaves and the Dirty Ground

was the first song our band learned to only barely play. I've just seen
a delivery man in a back brace. Do you think that might help you
get up, stay up in your daytimes? Or to try and lie stiller at night?
His uniform is the shade of the sea at the cove

the day we found a dead homing pigeon on the pebbles.
We memorised the number on the tag on its leg (the French
for heel is talon), stuffed some litter in our lifejackets and swam
back to the boat. When we called the number, did the fancier

say thank you? I think he did, I think he was grateful, I think
he'd been wondering where the bird had got to and I don't mean
like a balloon race. Together we decided the cliff might have killed it,
it might have collided whilst admiring the view, all the blue.

Brook

It's so easy for me to imagine it I don't even have to try. It's why
I lost interest in the postcard maker. I hardly needed him anymore,
with his surfboard. I think he understood.   That view
is stamped on my brain already, clear as day, except the grass
in the foreground is so dark it could almost be dusk overturned.
He told me the landslides are increasingly frequent, one for every
nice drop of rain. And so the cliff slips and the houses get closer
to the edge of it and the cliff gets weaker and so it goes on, and so
I take my love and I take it down. I think my mind's eye is in my gut.
The lifeboat house is so low now it looks like a bunker, some kind
of air-raid shelter, to be on the safe side twice over. Little does it
know.   The sunset takes longer these days, of course, with
further to go and less to hide behind.   I'd give a whole limb to be
there again. I'd know the right-handed cliff anywhere, with its slow
morning stretch, its curve, its crumble. Then there's the section
where clay turns to chalk and the peregrines were nesting last time.
Elsewhere, we'd lost a good chunk of car park, and the seagulls didn't
know where to land. Have you ever seen tarmac carried out to sea?
Like a jagged black ode to Noah's Island?   It was not good
news at all. May it never appear in a photo.

Nonina

If I am to know what I have been told, I cannot please
all the people all the time. That's fine. They don't
deserve what they get anyway, and yet we always let
them get away with it – that much obliging part of me,
that most optimistic canary that sings its heart out before
its supper, whose sweet sweet forewarnings go misunderstood.

I know a thing or two, three, four about music. It's my understanding
that we aren't alone on our instruments, and I am so eager to please.
My first CD was ten female blues singers, who could the one man be?
My baby don't, my baby don't, my baby just, my baby don't, my baby don't
I wondered what's wrong with baby, blinked, saw the fault lay with me,
that the voice was a woman's, not yet as low as they would let

her go, but not far off and seldom far from it. A prodigal alto starlet
asking nicely, clearly, then less so, but was wilfully misunderstood.
Oh Lord, I thought, this is Nina, and not the first introduced to me–
there's also my late great-grandmother, well-rested in peace
by the time I was born. Now I wear her dresses. No I didn't
know her, but I know she would smoke whilst lying in bed

tapping the cigarette out of the window. Poor Mr Walker below
always pruning the roses: a hat full of ash by breakfast-time. Don't let
me digress. I know a woman who can breathe in circles. Don't believe
me? Buy her CDs, or watch her on stage, standing
strong, silk dress and saxophone. Eyes closed, mouth open, poised,
regal, ready. She was so much to live up to, she wanted to teach me

everything she knew and everything she knew was too much for me,
honestly. And now she tours the world, but wherever she may be
I remember her practising, eight hours a day, the hundreds of pieces
of music in her two-room home above a vet's surgery. In lessons
I did my best to be half as capable, beautiful, completely understood
why the dogs howled to hear her, with one breath, bring the whole
house down.

There's a certain kind of light and no Nina, you're right, people don't
know what it's like to love somebody *don't let them take me,*
don't let them handle me and drive me mad baby, you understand
me now, don't you, no Nina, Nina no one alive can always be
an angel, or dead. When you hear the voice of an angel, don't let
them take you unless they move you and it's thrilling and it pleases

you, you who worked your whole life to be lived in pieces
(once more with feeling: *I've got life, I've got my freedom*),
yes Nina, you do and yet in your life you had to let
them take it away, drive you mad. We had a corner for instruments
at home – systems of sound all around the sound system. Your CD
played and I sat cross-legged and wondered what Mississippi

had done wrong. I was Little Miss Apprehensions,
wondering why this voice swore, pressing pause,
rewinding, wondering who all these babies could be.
I've got my man, I've got life. No Nina, you don't
have to treat them as one and the same thing, it struck me
I had listened long enough in time, so I struck my note albeit

from a second-hand Yamaha saxophone – it an alto, I a starlet
in my dreams at least, stabbing in the darkness at empathy,
because I'd seen so little and listened to so much. Believe me,
Nina, you did it your whole life, but we can't please
all the people all the time. That's why I try but I can't
bear to hear your voice break in your intro before

you cover *Who Knows Where the Time Goes* on Black Gold. Why
Nina, you count for yourself. You know Nina, always always you
knew all along what became of each beat, all on that day, didn't you,
do you understand me now, yes Nina, yes yet no Nina, I don't

Giddy

We missed a rabbit hole by inches as if
by magic that day galloping at one hell of a clip

along the clifftop from Shalcombe to Freshwater
and had we fallen we would really have fallen

his leg broken and maybe mine too   two birds
in flight felled by one fine faulty bone but we missed it

by a hare's breath and is it any wonder
when the land made way for a whale in its coastline

and stores its dinosaurs underground for safe-keeping
but takes them out onto the beaches when the weather is fine

I can't explain the homescape but imagine it often
describing where I'm really from to anyone who'll listen

searching high and low for any kind of wilderness
with little or no joy so far

but that day even the hang-gliders could not keep up
with us try as they might kicking their feet behind them

in the air I'm telling you the gorse-bushes
flowered as we jumped them and when we saw the woods

ahead and the trees slowed us down we came to
a standstill and the low mist mixed with the steam

from the sweat on his neck and we were not tired
we were only ethereal and we have never been further

Acknowledgements

Many thanks to the editors of the following journals where versions of two poems first appeared: 'Rocinante is no name for a skateboard' in *Magma: The Comedy Issue*, and 'The Stirrups' in *Foothill: A Journal of Poetry*.

Epigraph is taken from Thylias Moss, 'The Rapture of Dry Ice Burning Off Skin as the Moment of the Soul's Apotheosis', in *Rainbow Remnants in Rock Bottom Ghetto Sky* (Persea Books, 1991).

My gratitude also goes to: my friends, my aforementioned family, Timothy Donnelly, Dorothea Lasky, Deborah Paredez, Alan Gilbert, Mark Bibbins, Richard Howard, Luke Kennard, Caroline Sheldon, Bohdan Piasecki, Amy Dickson, The Hungarian Pastry Shop, The Putney High School Poetry Festival, Writers' Bloc.

Special mention, in the poems and here, to: Amy Winehouse, The Rolling Stones, Joni Mitchell, Aretha Franklin, Queen, The Eurythmics, The Cure, Sandy Denny, Dobie Gray, Bob Marley, The White Stripes, Fleetwood Mac and Nina Simone.